Life's Little Ahas

Life's Little Ahas

Things I Wish I'd Known

Rob Roseman

HARLAN
PUBLISHING

Life's Little Ahas

Harlan Publishing
www.bookpublishing4u.com

ISBN: 0-9772483-2-1

Library of Congress Catalog Number: 2005935979

Printed by Bang Printing Company, Brainerd, Minnesota USA

Acknowledgments

This book could not have been created without the input, assistance, support, and ahas of many people. I would like to acknowledge a few of them here.

My daughters Carrie and Sammie have taught me at least as much as I have taught them over the years, probably making them the biggest contributors to my personal repository of life's little ahas, though most of them are held in my heart, rather than between the pages of this book. Carrie and Sammie, I love you both very much.

Carrie has also been my sounding board and administrative support on this project, a role that has helped me view her as more than my daughter, but also as the bright and talented young woman she is.

Great appreciation goes out to artist Victoria Kwasinski, who created the front cover art and illustrations throughout the book. Your images so completely capture the humor and wisdom of the quotes that they often produce either gut level laughs or deep sighs. Thank you for that.

Thank you, Melanie Mulhall, editor, friend and copywriter, for helping me sort the wheat from the chaff and give form to the quotes, for capturing my voice in the writing, and for your enthusiastic support of the project.

Moneca Sheldon helped me get on the right road to success and showed me how to travel down that road. I am eternally grateful for that.

Patty, my girlfriend, patiently put up with me during the months while *Life's Little Ahas* was being created, believing in the importance of the project because she believes in me. If there is anything in life better than that, I am hard pressed to imagine it.

Finally, a thank you to all those friends, neighbors, relatives, co-workers, and acquaintances, who contributed the quotes without which this book could not have been possible. They include: Trish Barron, Cindy Burgess, Vera Roseman, Diane, Julie, Aimee, Joanne, Howard, Melanie, Steve, MaryEllen, Leon, Mam, Tom, James, Jan, Jaime, Khelsy, Mike, Richard, Kenda, JoAnn, Donna, Debi, Silja, Leit, Marty, Peggy, Katie, Phil, Stephen the Artist, Ann, Rich, Tom, Craig, Paula, Brandon, Rhonda, Leah, Chris, Don, Mary, Bruce, Sarah, Barbara, Jeff, Stephanie, Connie, Dorothy, Kipp, Nolan, Kimberly, Mary Anne, Dee, Celeste, Shanna, Karen, Rich C., Kathy, Carol, Jeff, Alice, Anjie, Ann, Beverly, Toni, Cecil, Ellen, and Ryann, Hal and Doug.

Introduction

Twenty-five years after giving up a life dream, I did some serious soul searching. What had happened? How had I managed to spend the last twenty-five years living for everyone else and starving my soul in the process?

In 1979 I was a rising star in the media, a popular and well-respected television Meteorologist at KUSA in Denver, with a movie and a handful of nationally run commercials to my credit. I had recently married and felt I was living my personal version of the American Dream. How quickly our dreams can vaporize!

Before long, I accepted a great opportunity with a Hartford, Connecticut station and we moved to the east coast. A glimmer of understanding began to settle into my young wife's mind. My career as a Meteorologist would always require us to relocate with opportunity. However, her version of the American Dream was me working in a business in her home town. There was a major disconnect between our dreams. We compromised. We returned to Denver, but I did not return to the television work I loved. Instead, I began a weather consulting business, something that would not require periodic relocation.

It could be argued that compromise is the act of two people sacrificing what they really want for an outcome that pleases neither. I believed that sacrificing my personal dream would ensure a happy marriage. It did not. Neither of us was happy and the marriage made its last gasp after 16 years.

Ten years later I looked over my shoulder to see the litter of a misspent life. I had done what I felt was good and right, what I needed to do to survive and make others happy, but *I* was not happy. When I realized that I had, in fact, stopped dreaming and was just living day to day, I took the time to excavate my feelings and recover a sense of what lights me up. I had more than a few ahas in the process.

One of those ahas was the realization that what I really missed about television was the fun of working in full public view, informing, assisting, and entertaining people. I no longer wanted to be a television Meteorologist, but I did want to reclaim that sense of living out my personal dream.

Another of those ahas was the insight that my ten-year-old fantasy of writing a book was really another path to fulfilling my dream of being in the public eye in a way that would benefit people. There is something heartening when you realize, in your fifties, that you were right at the age of twenty when you believed that the world was full of possibilities.

The ahas kept coming, in part because I was on the lookout for them. I began contemplating not only all the things I might have been right about at the age of twenty, but also all the things I wish I'd known at twenty that I understood now. I began to ask others, friends and acquaintances alike, about their insights into life, their own ahas. I took notes because the exploration was fun and many of the observations people shared with me were either funny or enlightening or both.

Before long, I realized I need not contemplate what to write a book about because I *had* a book…in all of those ahas, both my own and those shared by others. Further, I believed it fit my criteria of being informative, helpful, and entertaining.

A friend of mine believes that we go through life not getting it, not getting it, not getting it…getting it, and then dying about five minutes later. I cannot promise that this little book of ahas will increase your lifespan; I cannot even promise that it will increase the speed at which you bump into your own personal version of truth. But I can promise that you will most likely smile, chuckle, nod in agreement…and maybe even get a bit of enlightenment from it. That is my heart felt wish. If it inspires a few ahas of your own, all the better. I hope you will share them with me if it does.

Rob Roseman
Denver, Colorado
September, 2005

Life is what's arriving, not what has come and gone.
Read on. . . .

One thing I have learned in life is that if I want people to listen to me, I should never use the four words no one wants to hear: "I told you so."

Diane, 43

I have always said I would live my life differently if I had the chance to do it again. With age came the realization that once is enough.

Julie, 52

Our mothers are experts at pushing our buttons; after all, they were the ones who installed them.

Aimee, 53

When I was born, everyone around me was smiling as I was crying. My goal is to live my life in such a way that, at the end of it, I am the one who is smiling while everyone around me is crying.

Joanne, 57

I worked for JC Penney Company where they said the customer is always right. It drove me nuts, so I went into police work where the customer is always wrong.

Howard, 46

Narcissists never have a catharsis.

Steve, 53

I should have started saving for plastic surgery at birth.

Maryellen, 34

Experience is a wonderful thing; gaining it is the part I wish I could have skipped.

Leon, 56

In life, as in driving a car, it is wise not to back up too far.

Pat, 54

If you want to get back on your feet, just skip a couple of car payments.

Mam, 24

We live our lives as if somebody is keeping score when, in reality, no one is.

Tom, 52

Never regret what you've done in the past; at the time it was what you wanted.

Sammie, 15

I wish I had known sooner that you cannot change other people.

Rob, 52

What gives life meaning is being connected, being open and compassionate.

As a firefighter for 15 years, I arrived at yet another accident scene. But this one was different. I was riveted by the sight of a mother standing alone, devastated by grief, crying as her son was being tended to by ten emergency crew members. The boy was obviously dead and I was struck by how much attention was being given to a dead body while the mother was left alone in grief. I went over to her and just listened compassionately. In that moment, I was defined. . . this was my calling. . . to work in way where I could connect, be open and show compassion. That is, after all, what life is about.

James, 53

If I knew now what I knew then,
I wouldn't know much at all.

Jan, 51

Finally, I'm learning to trust the process of life.

Jamie, 53

If you think life is short, see if you can do anything that takes longer.

Anonymous

The only place where success comes before work is in the dictionary.

Khelsy, 15

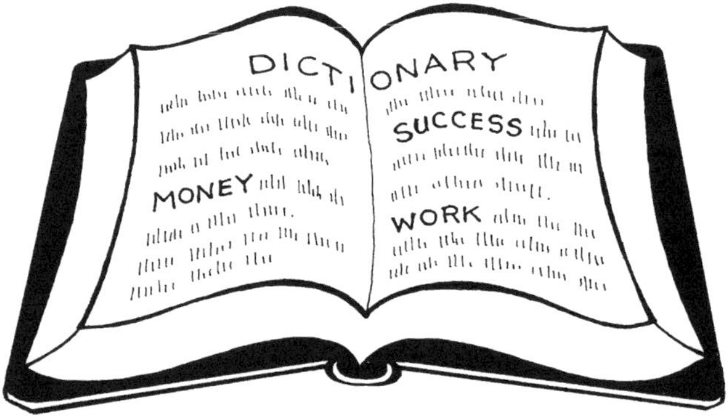

The dictionary is the only place you will find money appearing before work.

Rob, 52

Nobody sets out to make a wrong decision, but sometimes it just turns out that way.

Mike, 45

I am never in doubt, but frequently in error.

Jan, 51

When someone new lets you know who they are, believe them.

Richard, 55

You wouldn't be concerned about what people think of you if you knew how rarely they actually do.

Kenda, 42

Good friends are like stars and planets. You don't always see them, but you know they are always there.

Steve, 53

A best friend is like a four leaf clover, hard to find and lucky to have.

Anonymous

How is it that one careless match can start a forest fire, but it takes a whole box to start a campfire?

Anonymous

If you ask a question, you might be a fool for five minutes, but if you don't, you might be a fool forever.

Anonymous

Appreciate what money can buy, but value what it can't.

JoAnn, 53

Take care of your body. If you don't, where will you live?

Donna, 45

Who Exactly Are "They" Anyway?

Rob, 52

Sometimes being in the majority just means that all the fools are on the same side.

Anonymous

We all must dance to a tune and while it may not always be the tune we want, it is the tune we have, so dance we must. . . .with joy.

Debi, 45

Cherish yesterday, dream about tomorrow, live today.

Don, 57

If you want to see God laugh, just tell him your plans.

Pat, 54

You will never have it all together.

Anonymous

When children are involved, divorce is 'til death us do part, too.

Silja, 31

Education is taught in the classroom and learned outside it.

Bruce, 45

Maybe the end to something is the impetus for a new beginning.

Victoria, 48

Very often people don't know what's good for them.

Marty, 62

Character is who you are when no one is looking.

Steve, 53

When choosing those with whom you want to associate, look for those who can think and who care.

Peggy, 43

Everything I ever did seemed like a good idea at the time.

Stephen, 55

If someone would have just given me an instruction book for life, I could have saved a great deal of time and grief.

Ann, 49

The only difference between a rut and a grave is the depth.

Anonymous

Health is merely the slowest possible rate at which one can die.

Anonymous

If we all knew that everyone else is just as afraid as we are, we would relax and enjoy life's journey more.

Rich, 43

Beware of someone who would rather climb a tree backwards than tell the truth.

Tom, 68

Just because you know how to do something doesn't mean you will actually do anything with that knowledge.

Anonymous

Water and people have one thing in common: both seek their own level.

Craig, 58

Politics is supposed to be the second oldest profession. I have come to realize that it bears a very close resemblance to the first.

Anonymous

If you don't say anything they can't misunderstand you.

A New Orleans official, Sept. 13, 2005

It is said that God is a comedian playing to a very serious audience.

Richard, 56

One thing I don't like about Karaoke is sitting through the auditions.

Howard, 67

I will carry a gun, I will Cary Grant, but I will not Karaoke.

Howard, 67

If I had known that grandkids would be so much fun, I would have just skipped the kids part.

Stephen, 55

You cannot get to where you are going if you do not know where you are or if you refuse to take a step forward.

Melanie, 56

I wish I had listened to what everyone was trying to tell me when I was in a bad relationship. If I had, I would have gotten out sooner.

Rob, 52

When arguing about money, women admire a good loser.

Marty, 24

God really does have a sense of humor. He put man and woman together, didn't He?

Jamie, 53

It requires a very unusual mind to undertake the analysis of the obvious.

Steve, 53

Grandparents and grandchildren get along so well because they both dislike the same people.

Richard, 56

My management style is easy going and friendly, although there is a time for being autocratic: Monday through Friday from nine to five.

Howard, 52

If I'd known that marriage was 'til death us do part, I would have waited until I was closer to death to get married.

Dee, 56

I wish I had known that it's not the hand you are dealt, but how you play it.

Paula, 70

Today is the tomorrow you worried about yesterday.

Brandon, 16

I finally realized that when weeding, the best way to make sure you are removing a weed and not a valuable plant is to pull on it. If it comes out of the ground easily, it is a valuable plant.

Anonymous

No matter how hard you try, you can't control your heart.

Carrie, 22

I often fear the thing I want the most.

Anonymous

Never love anything that can't love you back.

Vera, 76

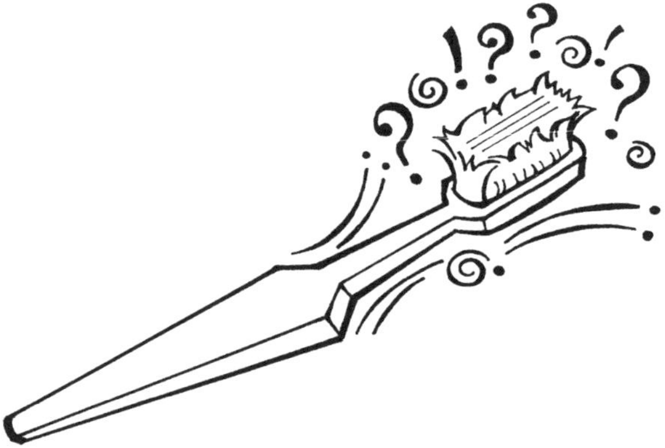

One of the toughest decisions to make is when to discard a toothbrush.

Marty, 24

Listen more to what people don't say than what they do say.

Rhonda, 33

Wishful thinking is not revelation; ego is not insight.

Melanie, 56

The key to success is self confidence; the key to self confidence is preparation.

Don, 57

The biggest lie on the planet is that you will be happy when you get what you want.

Anonymous

If I could invent just one thing, it would be reverse gravity. . . .for women.

Mary, 49

Life is not a video; no matter how hard you try, you can't rewind.

Aimee, 53

If you focus too much on the destination, you will forget to enjoy the journey.

Steve, 53

Age is a very high price to pay for maturity.

Steve, 53

When I was younger, I thought in terms of black or white, but the older I get, the grayer I get.

Suzanne, 56

Whenever I feel blue, I start breathing again.

Anonymous

Marriage is the leading cause of divorce.

Craig, 58

The greatest achievement is not to avoid failing, but to rise up again every time you do.

Don, 57

I'm constantly amazed by people who exchange one bad habit for another.

Leit, 31

Instructions on becoming a millionaire: Become a billionaire, then get married.

Richard, 56

As I solve one problem, I grow into another.

Bruce, 45

Without our rationalizations, where would we be?

Marty, 62

The easiest way to find something lost is to buy a new one.

Anonymous

Your head is a dangerous neighborhood; don't go in there by yourself.

Jamie, 53

Looking good guarantees you will not see anyone that night, but looking bad guarantees you will see everyone.

Sarah, 22

No one can ruin your day without your permission.

Anonymous

I wish I knew why people conversing in English often apologize for cursing by saying, "Excuse my French."

Rob, 52

If you wonder what you wanted out of life, look at what you have now.

Marty, 62

Selling begins when someone says, "No."

Phil, 46

The minute you start talking about what you are going to do if you lose, you have already lost.

Don, 57

The truth will set you free, but first it will really tick you off.

Anonymous

I wish I'd listened to my mother about the type of men I should date.

Barbara, 52

If you could trade your problems for those of anyone else, you would probably choose to keep your own.

Rob, 52

What hurts in the short term can help you in the long term.

Sarah, 22

When we no longer fear death, we can truly begin to live.

Marty, 62

When you find yourself in a hole, stop digging.

Chris, 39

Never look back with regret; look ahead with anticipation.

Don, 57

The people who tend to be the most successful in business are the most perseverant.

Jeff, 64

I would have saved all that stuff I have been giving away for years if I had realized I could have been selling it on EBay.

Maryellen, 34

To handle yourself, use your head. To handle others, use your heart.

Steve, 53

Growing old is mandatory, growing up is optional.

Vera, 76

I don't have to attend every argument I am invited to.

Anonymous

Being interested is just as important as being interesting.

Stephanie, 39

Here's the problem with people: we're always comparing our insides with other people's outsides.

Peggy, 43

Courage is not being fearless but overcoming fear.

Don, 57

A man who does not have a good relationship with his mother is not going to treat YOU very well, either.

Rob, 52

At some point, I finally realized that all the things I wished people had told me, they actually had . . . but I wasn't listening at the time.

Connie, 54

If you think you might be doing something wrong, you probably are.

Rob, 52

What they don't know doesn't scare me, but what they know for sure that is just plain wrong scares the heck out of me.

Mike, 45

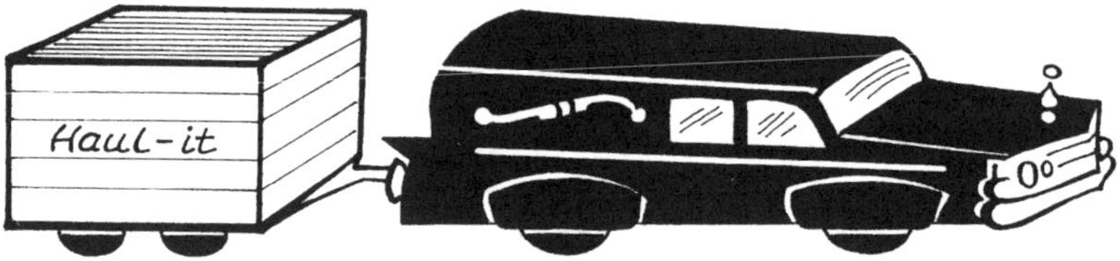

If you think you can take it with you, ask yourself if you have ever seen a hearse pulling a moving van.

Cindy, 52

You will only be as happy as you decide to be.

Anonymous

Isn't it amazing that in my lifetime there is a book packed with so much wisdom!

Dorothy, 90

Join the Fun! Send Us Your Own Ahas!

If you have any funny, serious, or thought provoking quotes to contribute to sequels of *Life's Little Ahas*, I would love to hear from you. Please send them to either the postal or email address below. Include your name, age, and a statement of release for their use in print or electronic sequels to this book.

Thank you.

Rob Roseman
Life Freedoms, Inc.
8691 E. Dry Creek Rd. #823
Centennial, CO 80112

Email: author@LifesAhas.com
Website: http://www.Lifesahas.com

BOOK ROB FOR YOUR EVENT!

Rob Roseman is a seasoned speaker, offering both a light hearted and thought provoking approach to life using the wisdom offered through the quotes of the ordinary and extraordinary. To book him for your next event or for more information contact him at the website at www.lifesahas.com.

Rob Roseman
Life Freedoms, Inc.
8691 E. Dry Creek Rd. #823
Centennial, CO 80112

Email: author@LifesAhas.com
Website: http://www.Lifesahas.com

ORDER FORM

(You may also order online at www.lifesahas.com)

Name: ______________________________

Shipping address: ______________________________

City: ______________________ State: ________

ZIP: __________

Email address: ______________________________

Please send me _____ copies of *Life's Little Ahas* ($12.95)

Shipping: $3.00 for 1st book. Add $1.00 for each additional.

Colorado Residents add 4.1% sales tax Total: $ __________

Make check payable to Life Freedoms, Inc. and send to:
Life Freedoms, Inc.
8691 E. Dry Creek Rd. #823
Centennial, CO 80112

Credit Card Orders (please print legibly)

☐☐☐☐☐☐☐☐☐☐☐☐☐☐☐☐

Expiration Date

☐☐–☐☐

CV Code (on reverse of card)

☐☐☐

☐ Visa

☐ MasterCard

☐ AMX

____

Cardholder Signature